Commerce in India

A look at Business & Cultural Standards

Marcia Williams

Commerce in India

A look at Business & Cultural Standards

ISBN-10:0-9983663-0-7
ISBN-13:978-0-9983663-0-2

About the Author

*M*arcia Williams is one of the co-Founders of Williams and King Publishers, and as of the publishing of this book, serves as the President.

Marcia is also the Co-Founder of Rhema University, Orlando, Florida. There she served as Assistant Vice President, bringing quality Christian post-secondary education from a Bachelor's level to the Doctorate level.

She has several business accomplishments which also includes owning one of the largest commercial, minority owned insurance agencies in Central Florida from early 1980s to mid-2000s. She also serves as Vice President of The Orlando Renaissance Writers' Guild.

Marcia has her Master's degree from Liberty University in Executive Development and her Bachelor's degree in Business Management from Oral Roberts University. She is the mother of three.

Table of Contents

Introduction

India is a South Asian country, the seventh largest country by measurement of area and the second largest by population and it is the most populous democracy in the world with over 1.2 billion people with 52% work in the agriculture industry (Anonymous, 2014). After nine decades of British rule, India got their independence on August 15, 1947 (Anonymous, 2014). Amidst the colorful array of pluralism, a vibrant culture, picturesque geographical terrain, this country continues to thrive at social, economic and political development.

According to the United Nations, India is on track to becoming the most populous country in the word by 2029 (Sreenivasan, 2009). This presents challenges for India in all areas of their structures as there are current social, political and economic challenges they have yet to successfully address in order to continually compete on a global scale and support an estimated 1.6 billion by 2029. There have been some

1

successes for example, progresses made due to their association with Brazil, Russia, China and South Africa (BRICS). The government will need to do a thorough evaluation of all economic segments, including foreign business protocols, in order to successfully facilitate both foreign and local businesses, to be poised and ready to support such population growth.

Chapter One

Economic History

India's economic history of economic growth can be classified in several phases. The first is immediately after independence, the economy was divided into public and private sectors (Gosai, 2013). At this time the private sector owned small, medium businesses and government controlled industries. In an attempt to improve the infrastructure, the government's position was to provide advancement of the current models of transportation (airlines, railways and public transportation), radio and television broadcasting, education and healthcare. However, due to government bureaucracy and corruption the progress has been slow.

3

In the 1970s under the presidency of Indira Ghandi, there was no economic advancement as her party was more interested in getting re-elected, and eliminating many of her opponents.

In the 1990s the economy continued a downward spiral with growing inflation, unemployment, poverty and a low international currency exchange rate. When the Soviet Union collapsed in 1991, this further negatively affected India because the Soviet Union supplied most of India's oil and consequently they, India, had to buy oil from the free market at a premium. Another event which hindered economic progression happened during the Gulf War. India was receiving huge allowances in foreign exchange from those citizens who were working in Iraq and other Middle Eastern countries. When the war started they were then sent home and India's foreign exchange reserve fell to an all-time low, enough to only support two weeks of imports. Under Prime Minister Narasimha Rao, the country began the economic reformation in the early 1990s. He lowered tariffs levels, revalued the currency, loosened the laws on industrial licensing and foreign direct investment policy. As a result, India became attractive to multinational corporations and international investors (Gosai, 2013).

The driving forces behind the economic growth can be identified in three segments: first, increased foreign investment (the United States being India's largest investment partner), second India's expertise information technology (Anonymous, 2011). Third, jobs generated from foreign direct investments and the rapidly growing information technology sector, stimulated a growing middle class which increased domestic consumption and in turn resulted in more foreign direct investments to meet the demands of the nationals. Due to the highly talented technical workers in a knowledge based economy, India continues to experience tremendous growth in various business administration areas such as medical billing, call centers and other business administration tasks. India's economy is now supported by its own expertise in information technology with major growth in the software sector, larger capital market, improving infrastructure and growing middle class with increasing disposable income (Gosai, 2013).

International Organizations

India is currently considered to be one of the fastest-growing economic powers in the world, thanks to the liberalization of 1991 which ushered in its spectacular economic progress over the last 20 years (Rienda, Claver & Quer, 2011). India and the United States (U.S.) share membership in a variety of international organizations, including the United Nations of which India is a member of the Security Council, the G-20, Association of Southeast Asian Nations (ASEAN) Regional Forum, International Monetary Fund, World Bank, and World Trade Organization. India is an ASEAN dialogue partner, an Organization for Economic Cooperation and Development partner under its Enhanced Engagement program, an observer to the Organization of American States, a member of the Indian Ocean Rim Association (IORA), of which the United States is a dialogue partner and BRICS (Brazil, Russia, India, China, and South Africa) (EUROSTAT, 2012).

The BRICS countries which include the largest developing markets in the world, owning 40% of the world's population between them. Similarities in economic conditions prompted an establishment of closer relationships to promote and ease the some of the constraints of trade and global economic hurdles (Eurostat, 2012). In addition, the development of this union between these emerging economies represent a shift in economic powers away from the traditional global economic leaders. They started with the initial desire to provide a strong counterpoint (in a certain sense, almost a challenge) to the dominant role played by the U.S. and the dollar (Scaffardi, 2014), triggered by the failing health and shortcomings in some of the global financial institutions.

Chapter Two

Locals Conducting Business

The magnitude of any culture is measured by the dimensions of the traditions which perpetuate the culture, namely; religion, communication, ethics, values and attitudes, manners, customs, social structures and education.

Religion

India has long been known for their diversity in religions. It is therefore very likely to have several different religions in one gathering, such as the work place. The Indian people have become very tolerable to such religious diversities, therefore a work environment with wide variety of religious beliefs should not cause controversy. Hinduism (started over 3,500 year ago), is the official religion of the country. Other religions which developed about 500 B.C are Buddhism and Jainism. Today, a little more than one percent is active in these religions. Hinduism, Buddhism and Jainism are considered to be the molders of the Indian philosophy. Sikhism was instituted in the 15th century of which about 2 percent of the Indian population participate. Islam and Christianity and are the largest segments on non-Indian religions of which Islam has about 12% of followers and Christianity about two and a half percent (Berger, 2014). The greatest religion influence in business and politics is Hinduism.

Hinduism. The major religion and the official religion of India is Hindu with about 83% of the population being active participants (Berger, 2014). It developed as the result of the Aryan tribes who migrated from central Asia around 1500 B.C. and inhabitants of India, the Harappans (Satterlee, 2009). Hindu is a combination of the major theological ideologies from both of these groups; from the Aryans it was polytheism and from the Harappan, sanctity of fertility.

According to Satterlee (2009), the Aryans developed the caste system as follows:

1. Brahmins or priests.

2. Kshatriyas or the king-warrior class.

3. Vaishyas which include merchants, farmers, laborers and crafts men.

4. Harijahns or the "untouchables". This class was extremely poor and discriminated against.

The higher the caste an individual is in, the more benefits and opportunities are available.

Hindus believe that a human can be reincarnated many times and his or her behavior will determine in which caste they will be re-embodied, thus there is not much charity as if a person is in a lower caste, as he or she is deserving of such a status because of deeds in their previous life.

Hinduism   incorporates various theological perspectives in that one has the option whether to be polytheistic, monotheistic, pantheistic agnostic or atheistic. The paths to attain salvation are based on rituals, the way of knowledge (realization of reality and self-reflection and devotion to the god one has chosen to worship).

Education

Over the years times have changed in India. What was once only available to the privileged in terms of progressive and higher education, is now more widely available. The education threshold has been steadily rising. A high school diploma is now even the requirement for lower paying jobs. English is taught at beginning in elementary school, preparing them for integration in the business arena which now is highly influenced with western investors and contracts for exports of goods and services to western cultures (Banerjee, Rangan, Vinayak & Muley, 2007). However, statistics prove that the English language proficiency is more than seven times higher among urban compared to rural schoolchildren (Anonymous, 2011). The average years of schooling are lowest in these most distant rural locations; reading, writing and computation ability are also lower; and

11

English language proficiency is all but non-existent (Banerjee, et al, 2007). For this reason, the sake of a better education for their children, parents from rural communities have a tendency to migrate to more developed cities. However, better education is growing rapidly in some rural areas, and when this generation of bucolic school aged children become parents this handicap to upward social mobility should become smaller.

English. Twenty-five years ago and before, there were no technical specialties with English. There were no sub-terms and no focus on technical communication. Today, due to the many industries and commerce with western influences and the boom of the exponential growth in the in area of information technology, several sub terms for English have evolved. People have started specializing in Communicative English, Business English, Technical English, Legal Writing and into the varied aspects of linguistics (Scaffardi, 2014). Examples of technical writing include designing the context for product brochures, technical descriptions, user manuals and various business type correspondences. The dependence of Information Technology (IT) companies on onsite and offshore structures with delivery of twenty-four-hour delivery support, demands individuals with precise language skills, the results being the need for and the learning of technical English spreading quickly. Hiring third party service agencies or individuals to teach their employees technical English is not uncommon. Some companies even go as far as to have in-house trainers and facilities specially designed for this purpose.

Engineering. Although higher education is offered in all fields such as liberal arts, medical, agricultural, engineering colleges serve as the 'gateway' institutions to degrees which many Indians perceive as a way to achieve a professional high paying job (Banerjee, et al., 2007). Even though an engineering degree does not automatically guarantee a high-paying job, nevertheless, a graduate from an engineering college is highly sought after and considered in high esteem. This is evidenced by the rapid growth of engineering colleges in India pursuant to the rise of the software industry, which is the largest

13

employer of graduates, offering a large and growing pool of well-paid positions (Bertrand, Rema, & Sendhil, 2010).

In the early 1980s, there were only about 100 engineering colleges in India, admitting fewer than 25,000 students each year. Since then, the number has grown apace, reaching nearly 1,600 colleges by 2010, collectively admitting over 500,000 students every year — the fastest expansion in any segment of India's higher education sector over the past thirty years (Banerjee, et al., 2007).

Today India has a large community of scientists, scholars and Indian researchers performing research in a wide variety of areas including science, technology, medicine, humanities and social sciences and their work is published in thousands of journals (Arunachalam, 2008). Of the many scientist and engineers that are trained in country, a large percent of the best graduates leave to further their education in western countries. According to Andrew White of Forbes Magazine, "India is the leader in sending its students overseas for international education exchange, with over 123,000 students studying outside the country and over 100,000 studying in United US

universities (White, 2007).

Chapter Three

Customs and Manners

Social Hierarchy. Religion, caste and language are the determining factors of social and political societies. The Hindu caste system dictates the social hierarchies to which individuals belong and has a huge influence on customs and manners. Societies are largely developed into thousands of jatis-local, endogamous groups based on occupation and organized hierarchically according to complex ideas of purity and pollution (Krishna, 2014). An individual's status is usually determined by the father's social class, income, occupational status or educational achievement. There exists a correlation between parents and children's socio-economic status: richer fathers tend to have richer children; poorer children tend to go together with poorer parents. Even though discrimination based on caste membership has been outlawed since the 1940s, it is still visibly evident especially in the rural communities. Therefore, the government has instituted affirmative action programs in an effort to curb this behavior. In addition, expanding education, land reform and economic opportunity through access to information, communication, transport and credit are helping to lessen the harshest elements of the caste system (Sethi & Rohini, 2010).

Customs. India's cultures are complex and different. At one time, only higher-caste women, like Indira Gandhi, can go to college and own businesses. However, some lower castes have been outperforming some of the higher caste members in social and political achievements.

Women are another segment in society which have been discriminated against. In some places, women must hide their faces behind veils and obey men absolutely. In other places, women are strong, independent, and outspoken. India embraces each extreme and many shades in between (Kanagasabapathi, 2007). Even today there

17

are many arranged marriages however, in some circles this is done with the consent of the bride and groom. Divorce is not looked upon kindly and women are particularly disgraced when they divorce their husbands. Even though laws have been passed to inhibit giving a dowry to the groom's family, it is still a common practice. The law prosecutes very few people for this crime.

Centuries of discrimination against women have led to the development of feminist activists' groups and organizations to help women. For example, Ela Bhatt who served as chairwoman of Women's World Banking and is one the board of the Rockefeller foundation, started the Self Employed Women's Association (SEWA). This organization lends small amounts of money to women who sell vegetables for 50 cents a day on the street, pick up scraps of paper for recycling, make cigarettes, and run other tiny businesses. Most of SEWA's 150,000 members are poor and illiterate, but the organization gives women hope.

A few additional customs and manners are; a person's head is considered sacred so it is an offense to touch someone's head, even a child's. It is also offensive to touch someone's shoes or feet as they are considered unclean. Indian men are not so concerned with their business attire, but they do expect their business counterparts to dress business appropriate (Andrea, 2012). Women should have their upper arms, back, chest are legs covered and wearing leather items could be offensive as Hindus hold certain animals in reverence. Guests should take off their shoes at the door before entering a household as is considered respectful and women tend to remain in the kitchen making sure the guests do not run out of food and drinks.

Hindus have a large respect for animals which is the reason so many of them are vegetarians. At meals, they offer food to god(s) as they believe food is very important to assist in an individual's lifestyle, and during meals it is acceptable to eat with your hands – just not the left hand as this is considered an offense. It is also offensive to eat or drink from another's plate, bowl or glass. Also, it is not uncommon for guests to invite other guests without a dinner invitation. The host is expected to behave welcoming. This is a sign of the warmth and the level of relationship between the host and the original guest(s). Indians are big on title so one should address each individual by their professional titles or "Mrs." and "Mr.".

Values and Attitudes

When evaluating values and attitudes the differentiation of values and norms must be made. Values and norms differ in definition whereas values are, for example, being monogamous in a marriage and norms are the expected behaviors from each individual in the marriage.

Evaluating values and attitudes in India is very difficult due to the huge diverse population, the many cities, towns and villages. Most of the population practice some form of spirituality which then becomes the base and source of an individual's values (Srinivas, 1993). These values carry over to their jobs, social circles and politics.

Values may differ from one town to the next and from one village to the next. There is a huge difference in values between those who live in the city and those who live in the rural and surrounding areas. The globalization of India's economy has caused an expansion of the middle class and this expansion has extended even to members of lower castes who would normally be subjected and regarded as being deserving of inferior treatment. As a result, some societies have been forced to integrate traditional values with more modern values. Traditional values are held stronger in the rural areas and sometimes the attempt to reform their value systems results without change.

In the more progressive communities and cities, changes in social values are becoming more and more accepted. Education of the middle class along with the influence from western cultures are the primary catalysts of value and norm changes. Women are now more educated than before and are able to obtain jobs as their male counterparts. Traditionally, in a home where the man is the sole income provider, at the displeasure of his wife's actions, he is allowed to beat her. Today, with the empowerment of women through education and the feminist activist groups, both males and females are faced with decision to go against the traditional values and norms or adjust to a new behavior system.

India is at a turning point where politicians and the public attitude towards corruption is changing.   In 2012 Anna Hazare, an anti-corruption activist, led a series of protests in an effort to make the government take notice and introduce legislature to curtail corruption, all to no avail. However, this movement brought the problem to the surface, increasing awareness among the nationals. Historically, few Indian politicians have been imprisoned on corruption charges. It has long been accepted that it is impossible to do business in certain sectors or in certain Indian states without paying bribes to government officials. But those practices are currently being frowned up by the United States and Britain who have anti-corruption laws in place which deal harshly with bribery (Srinivas, 1993). However, the Indian government has an uphill battle as certain levels of corruption have become engrained in the culture.

Chapter Four

Communication

India has more diverse languages than any other country, arguably, greater linguistic diversity than any other large country (Arunachalam, 2008). The 1961 census listed 1,652 languages, most of which were dialects and some have now died out, but the current amount of remaining dialects stand at today is well over 300 (Prasuna, 2012). The main original languages are Hindi, Bengali, Telugu, Marathi, Tamil and Urdu – spoken by more than 50 million people each. In 1952, Chatterji's article stated that Hindi was the national language (Chatterji, 1952), however opponents have argued that Hindi should be the national language and India, being heavily industrialized by western interest and so much business communication is done in English, which is considered the official language (Arunachalam, 2008).

In today's business economy whether locally or on a global scale, clear, precise, and fluid communication has been proven to be extremely important for organizations to conduct business on medians which will prove to be cost and time effective (Prasuna, 2012). Due to the infiltration and independence of the English language, even more of the local languages and dialects are in jeopardy of becoming extinct in the coming years. Nationals are speaking Communicative English, Business English and Technical English. This is primarily as a result of globalization, the industrial and agricultural revolution and the boom in the area of information technology (IT). The IT emergence of industry dominance thrives on onsite/offshore model of communications unlike many other countries (Prasuna 2012). In order to encourage and accommodate this shift, educational reforms emphasize the importance to learn English in schools, colleges and engineering institutes. Modernists agree that languages should be learned by speaking, listening or writing that particular language on a daily basis. This type of learning would of course need an environment conducive to such learning (Prasuna, 2012). So as a result, larger corporations even have in-house instructors to enhance workers' knowledge and skills of the English language. Many technical institutes, in addition to focusing on the technical components of the language, have included as a part of their curriculum courses on writing a business plan and proposal writing in an attempt to equip their potential managers with the skills necessary to compete on an international level.

However, in spite of all these attempts, the quality of the thousands of graduates' ability to communicate fluently and effectively in English is still, to a large measure, ineffective and has prevented many otherwise qualified individuals from gainful employment. Even though India has emerged on the economic national scene, an immense challenge remains on the most effective methods of teaching English in the rural schools as some schools are still using traditional methods. Efforts from both social and political advocates are often met with strong opposition, however, it does not change the fact that in order for India to continue to compete on a global level, changes to must be instituted to combat this issue. Researchers and politicians both agree that this is an area which needs improvement in order to attract not only more foreign investors, but also for foreign companies to hire more of the Indian nationals instead of relocating managers from their own countries.

Chapter Five

Ethics

"Religion plays a very poignant part in business ethics, more than some countries like China, therefore understanding how religion affects business and business ethics is essential to a foreign company looking to be successful in India", (Berger, 2014).

There is a distinct correlation between religious ethics and economics and a vast difference between eastern and western business ethics. However, young managers are shifting away from the old paradigm value system toward the more contemporary management style which includes emphasis on quality, learning and teamwork. (Chatterjee & Pearson, 2000). These influences are primarily seen in the urban and metropolitan cities, as the more rural citizens tend hold on to traditional business ethics. Critics agree that in order to be successful in the global economy, the ethical standards of the west must be adapted, thus the continual embracing of western values and influences on a national level (Lefebvre, 2011).

While western thought promotes the idea that action is propelled by individual drives, the Vedantic philosophy common in Indian views the role of personality with its internal predispositions for motivation, as secondary to societal considerations in guiding behavior (Chatterjee & Pearson, 2000). Therefore, someone who is ethical is someone whose behavior is acceptable according to what the norm which defines the standard of behavior. For example, if the standard is to accept a bribe to issue certain public utilities, this behavior will be taught to new employees and the locals would have accepted that this is the accepted behavior and standards to get their utilities. The efforts of trying to curb this behavior have been addressed by many local activist group, however certain behavior patterns have become a way of life for decades and is met with immense resistance to change. Thus when applying modern managerial theories and methodology to the Indian business or work environment, certain adjustments must be made to accommodate for differences in ethics.

Corruption

Corruption in India intersects every area of business and in the political arenas. India ranks 85 among 180 countries in the Corruption perception index of Transparency International. Transparency International India (TII), disclosed that in 2008 residents who lived below the poverty level were paying bribes to get 11 of the basic public services that they were already entitled to receive. TII also reveals that a truck driver delivering goods pays an estimate $1800 per year at check points, toll plaza and state boarders. The preceding illustrations are just examples of how much corruption has become embedded into their culture.

Cultural corruption has hindered many countries from doing business with India to where they slipped from eighth to fourteenth in receiving foreign direct investments (King, 2011). However, with

29

Britain and the United States introducing anti bribery laws, the Indian government has had very little choice but to become active in intervening this type of action.

When India integrated into the international economy, new operating processes, management and business systems emerged as a result of globalization, however ethics still deteriorated. Many critics blame the failure to abandon business ethics on old religious customs as one of the major causes, which also resulted in the deterioration of the economy.

Indian companies wishing to compete successfully on a global level cannot ignore worldwide changes in the area of business ethics. Competing to win in the global marketplace will require them to institute ethics and compliance policies that are at globally acceptable standards and build an ethical corporate culture by making ethics and values a prominent part of the leadership agenda (Berger et al., 2013a).

Chapter Six

Integrating the Elements by Locals

Religion

Business practices are heavily influenced by the predominant Hindu religion. In the workplace the multiplicity of religions ordinarily does not present a problem as India is very tolerant in its diversity of religious beliefs. Managers, must however acquaint themselves with certain religious ceremonies such as those for opening a new office and the ceremony for breaking ground for new buildings or other facilities. Additionally, employers must also be aware of the religious holidays of Hindu and Islam. Some holidays last several days so management must plan ahead to avoid production coming to a standstill or being offensive if businesses are closed during some sacred holidays.

Education

Since 1991, the Indian people have witnessed the dawn of their nation in a new economic climate. Significant efforts have and are still being made to improve the quality of not just technical English but also spoken English because more fluency will lead to more individuals to better jobs. An English curriculum can be found in many elementary schools, preparing young students for business life outside the Hindu linguistic communication. Lower caste members are now more informed of the need to pursue education in order to achieve a more prosperous life outside of their castes of societal dictation, thus more and more low caste members are migrating closer to urban and metropolitan cities for the sake of their children getting a better education. The middle class continues to educate their kids with an emphasis on higher education in medical or engineering areas of specialties while many Indian nationals still seek technical degrees in foreign countries as a way to return to their country and occupying a more prestigious corporate position along with higher pay.

Customs and Manners

Invitations to a meeting is usually done through oral communication as emails and letters are considered impersonal and may be ignored (Andrea, 2012). Meetings usually begin with coffee, tea and light conversation, usually about families and situations or individuals relating castes or politics. As opposed to meetings in the west, there is no agenda. During the meeting, hesitant answers are appropriate veils for an open "no" which would equal an offense and nodding of heads when listening to somebody does not mean agreement. t simply means they are paying attention (Andrea, 2012). Negotiations are usually left toward the end. Unlike some eastern cultures, Indians are very expressive in their negotiations and coming to a decision too early may be a bit daunting to them, because they were deprived the pleasure of their emotional manifestation, they may feel that something might be amiss. Indians like to negotiate with the long term in mind and will compromise for the sake of win-win results for all in the end. Contract modifications are common as they are not seen as an end, but the beginning of negotiations (Kanagasabapathi, 2007).

A few more items which could be of significance in a meeting are; as most Indians are vegetarians, meetings arranged with food is usually a vegetarian menu. Eating the meal takes place at the end of a meeting or hospitality session, so the hosts expects the guests to leave immediately after dessert. Staying afterwards would be considered impolite (Andrea, 2012).

Values and Attitudes

The type of organizational structure is generally a simple structure where the manager makes all material decisions. Subordinates rarely make decisions without the approval of their superiors so it is important to determine the manager, supervisor, owner or CEO as negotiation with others could prove to be as waste of time. This is the result of many of them being in the caste system and still adhere to the

34

hierarchy mindset. For example, upper management would never do a job if a lower ranked employee was available to do the job.

In fostering business relationships, it is recommended to allow the relationships to develop instead of pushing or forcing to make it happen. Indians value quality interpersonal relationships and pushing could damage the potential of the association. Decisions will be made not only based on facts, figures and an articulate presentation, however, Indians base their decisions on trust of the individuals, intuition and faith. A business decision is usually slow coming if trust has not yet been established.

Ethics

Business ethics is still highly influenced by ancient Indian practices and ethics, however, younger managers are trending toward more western management styles. This is met with some opposition especially when dealing with older employees and those directly from rural areas who have not yet been introduced to western ethical practices and behaviors. As the middle class expands, however western ethics are becoming more and more accepted as standard for business behavior. Managers will continue to face an uphill battle because the traditional Indian ethical practices still permeate their culture.

Communication

Everyday life in India is spoken mostly in the Hindu language but business in conducted in English. English is the official language of India, however there are still many hurdles to bring most Indians to the fluency level of the western countries operating business there. Despite the fact that there is a large pool of labor force, that percentage diminishes if there is a communication issue. Even though English is taught in urban and metropolitan schools, business conversational fluency remains a challenge. Some businesses have resorted to hiring independent individuals or companies to instruct their employees on the art of communicating fluently in English. Some even have in house instructors and designated areas as they have realized the importance of this issue.

It is also important to understand the non-verbal communication to effectively understand what is apparent but not spoken. A few examples are: bow with hands together when meeting someone, to call another person with your hand, the palm must face downward and even though handshakes have become more common women still generally refrain from physical touch with a man.

Chapter Seven

Comparing with US Culture and Business

India is 80% actively practicing Hindu with values which are based on their religion and traditions, while the United States is 80% Christianity with values which are Christian based with the morality code of tradition and society. When studying Hofstede's typology on the overall cultural diversities between these two countries, of the five cultural dimensions, two point to a degree of cohesion while three areas show quite a significant difference. India's score in Power Distance was twice as high as the United States and the U.S. scored twice as high in Individualism (LeFebvre, 2011). These results steer to the fact that employees in India, being in a culture where the caste system, even though abolished is still very much practiced, continue to work in a hierarchical structure which creates a business environment where all authority lies with the boss and employees are not generally empowered (LeFebvre, 2011). The hierarchy demands absolute obedience and commands that superiors be addressed by their titles. On the other hand, the business practices in the U.S. are becoming more and more individualistic and companies continue to find ways to empower employees in order to give them greater job satisfaction, job appreciation, loyalty and empowerment

In the U.S. communication is considered low-context which involves very detailed information and employees usually have access to upper management, whereas India's communication is high context where the unspoken or unread information can be interpreted based on culture. Employees must answer to their direct supervisor and circumventing direct supervisors is frowned upon, often met with disciplinary consequences. American managers tend to make decisions from an analytical perspective based on a code of conduct or professional ethical standards whether formal or informal, whereas

Indian business individuals base their decision making on context of the situation and intuition.

The Implications for US businesses
to Conduct Business in India

There are many challenges to doing business in India. Some of the elements that multinational corporations must consider are; doing business in an inadequate infrastructure, understanding their complicated tax system and rigid labor laws, complex judicial system and inefficient public delivery system afflicted by corruption. (Ray, 2011).

According to Mckinsey and Company report, "Building India: Accelerating Infrastructure Projects" (2009), projects awarded in national highways, power and port sectors fell short by 30% than the planned targets in the first two years of the current 11th plan". The government is continually making efforts to improving roads and the 150-year-old antiquated railway system however, one of the major problems has been access constraints global infrastructure construction companies have not yet been effectively responding to the global bids (Ray, 2009). Additionally, the turnaround time in the Indian Port is 3.6 days compared to 1.5 days in the United States. The former and the later issues will prevent the untimely delivery of merchandise, incur unnecessary fees and penalties, so adjustments or alternative plans will need to be considered.

The Indian tax system is complicated layered in many levels of state and government taxes. The cumulative incidence of indirect taxes on goods is estimated to be at 28% of the sale price without taxes (CCI, 2009). This can prove to be burdensome to a company.

In taking a look at the labor laws, a multinational corporation would have to carefully and strategically plan its workforce. The Industrial Disputes Act of 1947 make it difficult for a company that employees more than 100 workers, to lay off employees without the permission of a government authority, which can be difficult to give as trade unions are very aggressive in opposing this type of move. The law further dictates that even if the authority to lay off is granted, the company must begin layoffs with the last person to be hired in that category (Ray, 2011). As an alternative to layoffs in recession times, some companies have been downsizing by offering attractive voluntary retirement packages. A further analysis of India's of the pros and cons with specific challenges can also be ascertained by a SWOT (strengths, weaknesses, opportunities and threats) analysis.

* STRENGTHS	WEAKNESS
1. Agriculture	1. Very high percentage of workforce involved in agriculture which contributes only 17.2% of the Gross Domestic Product
2. High percentage of cultivable land	
3. Huge pool of labor force	
4. Huge English speaking population, availability of skilled manpower	2. Around a quarter of a population below the poverty line
5. Extensive higher education system, third largest reservoir of engineers	3. High unemployment rate
	4. Poor infrastructural facilities
	5. Low productivity
6. Rapid growth of IT and BPO sector bringing valuable foreign exchange	6. Hugh population leading to scarcity of resources
	7. Low literacy rates
7. Abundance of natural resources	8. Rural-urban divide, leading to inequality in living standards
8. Low wages	

OPPORTUNITIES	THREATS
1. Scope for entry firms in various sectors for business	1. Global economy recession/slowdown
2. Inflow of Foreign Direct Investment is likely to increase in many sectors	2. High fiscal deficit
	3. Threat of government intervention in some states
3. Huge population of Indian Diaspora in foreign countries (NRIs)	4. Volatility in crude oil prices across the world
	5. Growing Import bill
4. Huge domestic market: Opportunity for multinational corporations for sales	6. Population explosion, rate of growth of population still high
	7. Agriculture excessively dependent on monsoon
5. Vast forest area and diverse wildlife	
6. Huge agricultural resources, fishing, plantation crops	

This SWOT analysis was performed by Ankit Porwal, of Jain College of Engineering.

In addition to all the afore mentioned issues which needs to be considered, a multiplicity of clearances and approvals from both state and local governments are needed. According to Gautam Ray (2011), there are 24 clearances required depending on the industry and waiting for approvals could take an extended period of time due to customary delays or employees or officials expecting a payoff.

Incentives

Some of the incentives the government of India will grant to various size businesses are, power tariff (exemption from the payment of electricity duty), freeze on the tariff charged for new units for a few years after the start of a business, assurance of uninterrupted electricity supply and concessional rates of billing (Budhwar, 2001).

Other incentives are discounted loans granted by the government, price preference on goods made by Small Scale Industries on purchases made by government organizations and independent firms controlled by the government, exemption from the payment of the entry tax for a specified period of time, preferential allotment of land

and sheds in industrial areas and grants of interest free loans in lieu of deferred sales tax (Rienda, Claver & Quer, 2011).

Additionally, in order to encourage the cumbersome task of applications for approval to the many government agencies, a few states now offer streamlining the investment approval process by introducing common and centralized application forms for various approvals. A 'green channel facility', has been introduced in some states, where applications required for clearances will be received and processed through various institutional offices on a time bound basis.

India can achieve more sustainable growth, however a second generation of reformation will be required to improve financial and legal systems to protect investments, modernize the infrastructure and speed up privatization of government owned businesses. It is also important to revamp the business tax laws to reduce the tax liability, upgrade labor laws to the international business standards, and curb the extensive bureaucracy and corruption.

It is undeniable the success of some western companies in India today. Many multinational corporations are attracted to the huge labor force which comes with very low payroll, thus significantly increasing the company's bottom line. However, as this publication has outlined, there are many factors to consider when deciding to venture to the country of India. Time, money, marketing and education must be invested to study the various elements previously discussed, after which finding suitable candidates for the management positions in the country. This person must be one who, in additional of having the necessary management skills and experience, is adjustable and open in nature, able to understand and communicate fluently and one not easily offended and one who is a quick learner. There is a myriad of personality assessments available through the Human Resources department which can be utilized in finding individuals who are "the right fit". After careful and strategic planning, it is very possible to have a successful business in India.

References

Andrea, H. (2012). Good manners and their role in international business. *International Journal of Academic Research in Business and Social Sciences, 2*(4), 122-131.

Arunachalam, S. (2008, June). Open access in india: Hopes and Frusrations. In Proceedings ELPUB 2008 Conference of Electronic Publishing, Toronto, Canada.

Berger, R., Herstein, R., Jaffe, E. (2014) "The evolution of business ethics in India", *International Journal of Social Economics, 41 (11),* 1073 - 1086.

Banerjee, R., Vinayak, P. (2007) 'Engineering Education in India: Draft Final Report'. Mumbai: Observer Research Foundation, Energy Systems Engineering, IIT Bombay.

Bertrand, M., Rema, H., Sendhil M. (2010) 'Affirmative Action in Education: Evidence from Engineering College Admissions in India', *Journal of Public Economics* 94(1–2):16–29.

Budhwar, P. (2001). Doing business in india. *Thunderbird International Business Review, 43(4),* 549-568.

Chatterjee, S.R. and Pearson, C.A.L. (2000), Indian managers in transition: orientations, work goals, values and ethics", *Management International Review, (40)1,* 81-95.

Chatterji, S. (1952). Civilisations. *Institue De Sociologie De L' Universite de Bruxelles*. 2(1), 19-32.

Cohen, S. (2002). *India: Emerging Power*. Washington, DC. Brookings Institution Press.

Eurostat (2012). The European Union and the BRIC Countries. Luxembourg: Publications Office of the European Union.

Gosai, D. (2013). History of economic growth in india. *International Policy Digest.*

India. (2014). Washington: Superintendent of Documents.

King, I. (2011, Sep 06). India's attitude is changing. *The Times.*

Kanagasabapathi, P. (2007). Ethics and values in Indian economy and business. International Journal of Social Economics, Vol. 34(9), 577-585.

Krishna, A. (2014). Examining the structure of opportunity and social mobility in india: Who becomes an engineer? *Development and Change, 45*(1), 1-28.

LeFebvre, R. (2011). Cross-cultural comparison of business ethics in the U.S. and India: a study of business codes of conduct: *Journal of Emerging Knowledge on Emerging Markets* (3).

McKinsey & Company. (2009). Building India: Accelerating Infrastructure Projects [Report Leaflet].

Prasuna, M. G. (2012). Technical communication in india trends and concerns. *Theory and Practice in Language Studies, 2*(12), 2478 2482.

Porwal, A. (2014). SWOT analysis of indian economy. Jain College of Engineering.

Ray, G. (2011). Doing business in india: Opportunities and challenges. *Journal of Marketing Development an Competitiveness, 5*(4), 7795.

Rienda, L., Claver E., Quer D., (2011) Doing business in India: a review of research in leading international journals: *Journal of India Business Research, (3)3*, 192 – 216.

Sreenivasan, T. P. (2009). India at the united nations: More give than take. *India quarterly, 65*(4), 475-481.

Sethi, Rajiv and Rohini Somanathan (2010) 'Caste Hierarchies and Social Mobility in India'.

Srinivas, M. (1993). Changing values in India today. Economic and Political Weekly, 28(19), 933-938.

Scaffardi, L. (2014). BRICS, a multi-centre "legal network"? *Beijing Law Review, 5*(2), 140-148.

Transparency International India. (2009). India Corruption Study, 2008.

White, A. (2007). Indians flock to the united states. *Forbes*.

www.ingramcontent.com/pod-product-compliance
Lightning Source LLC
Chambersburg PA
CBHW060513220326
41598CB00025B/3647